D0837565

Also by Spike Milligan

THE BEDSIDE MILLIGAN

A DUSTBIN OF MILLIGAN

A BOOK OF BITS or A BIT OF A BOOK

MILLIGAN'S BOOK OF RECORDS

THE GREAT MCGONAGALL SCRAPBOOK (with Jack Hobbs)

THE BEDSITTING ROOM (with John Antrobus)

BADJELLY THE WITCH

DIP THE PUPPY

The Little Pot Boiler

*a book based freely
on his seasonal overdraft*

by

Spike Milligan

*

*Write your own title in space provided

Star

A STAR BOOK

published by

the Paperback Division of

W. H. ALLEN & CO. LTD

A Star Book
First Tandem Edition 1965
Reprinted 1965, 1966
Reprinted 1967 by Universal-Tandem Publishing Co. Ltd
Reprinted 1968 (twice), 1969, 1970, 1971, 1972, 1973 (twice),
1974 (twice), 1975, 1978, 1979
This edition reprinted 1980
by the Paperback Division of
W. H. Allen & Co. Ltd
A Howard and Wyndham Company
44 Hill Street, London W1X 8LB

First published in Great Britain by Dobson Books Ltd 1963

Copyright © 1963 by Spike Milligan

Printed in Great Britain by The Anchor Press Ltd, Tiptree, Essex

ISBN 0 352 30630 0

ACKNOWLEDGEMENTS

The publishers would like to express their sincere thanks to all those persons known or unknown who have wittingly or unwittingly helped in the making of this book.

DEDICATION

One gets few chances of thanking in print people one admires; therefore, I would like to dedicate this slim volume to Peter Scott and his companions for their efforts in trying to save the bird and the animal kingdoms from extinction.

Spike Milligan
May 18, 1963

From *HARRY SECOMBE*

Spike Milligan, soldier, poet, man of letters —he has five of mine he has not answered—came up the hard way, the lift was out of action.

I first met him in North Africa during the last war. I was laundering my white flag in a wadi when I became aware of being watched by a man wearing a German helmet, an Italian tunic and British boots.

"Don't believe in taking chances," he said, and I knew at once that here was a man after my own heart.

Our friendship ripened in the warm sun, and one day he confided to me that he had decided to become a writer. Shyly he shewed me a piece of paper with the word "NEVERTHELESS" on it.

"I'm going to write another word tomorrow," he said.

By the time the war had finished he had written over two hundred thousand words. Now came the great task of putting them all together. Walls had to be taken down all over the continent and carefully re-assembled in a disused banana factory in East Finchley.

Workmen tiptoed carefully through the Syntax, and eventually the gigantic undertaking was completed. The result you hold in your hand. Careful with it, now.

From PETER RAWLEY
(Actor-Manager)

Bearded funster Spike M., famed crypto-conservative and part-time Indian club juggler, completed this his third volume with the support. Some may discern nostalgic echoes of Catullus and indeed Moschus, in this quaintly neo-classical opus. Others may discover a vaguely symbolistic atmosphere in many of the lyrics. We've all got to make a living.

CONTENTS

The Little Pot Boiler

ONCE UPON

Once upon an unfortunate time, there was a hairy thing called man. Along with him was a hairier thing called animal. Man had a larger brain which made him think he was superior to animals.

Some men thought they were superior to men. They became leader men. Leader men said "We have no need to work, we will kill animals to eat." So they did.

Man increased, animals decreased. Eventually leader men said "There are not enough animals left to eat. We must grow our own food." So man grew food.

Now, the only animals man had not destroyed were tiny ones, like rabbits and mices, and these little animals were caught eating some of man's crops. "These animals are a menace. They must die."

In China they killed all the sparrows. In Australia they killed all the rabbits. Everywhere man killed all wild life. Soon there was none, and all the birds were poisoned. Leader man said "At last! We are free of pests."

Man's numbers increased. The world became crowded with men. They all had to sleep standing up. One day a leader man saw a new creature eating his crops. This creature's name was starving people.

"This creature is a menace!" said leader man . . .

CONTAGION!

Elephants are contagious!
  Be careful how you tread.
An Elephant that's been trodden on
  Should be confined to bed!

Leopards are contagious too.
  Be careful tiny tots.
They don't give you a temperature
  But lots and lots—of spots.

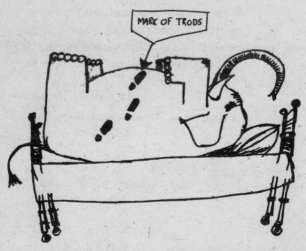

Confined-to-bed Elephant

The Herring is a lucky fish,
   From all disease inured.
Should he be ill when caught at sea;
   Immediately—he's cured!

THOMAS TALLIS

Thomas Tallis
Bore no man any malice
Save an organist called Ken
Who played his music rather badly
                        now and then.

To *ANTHONY WEDGWOOD BENN*
(without his permission)

Anthony Wedgwood Benn
Is one of the bravest of men,
The worst in life he can fear
Is ending it as a Peer!

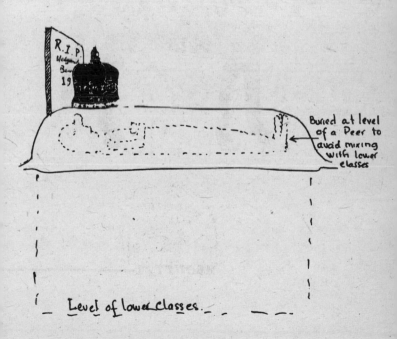

Buried at level of a Peer to avoid mixing with lower classes

Level of lower classes.

ABOUTTTT—————————————————

——————————— **TURN!**

THE ABC

T'was midnight in the schoolroom
And every desk was shut,
When suddenly from the alphabet
Was heard a loud "Tut-tut!"

Said A to B, "I don't like C;
His manners are a lack.
For all I ever see of C
Is a semi-circular back!"

"I disagree," said D to B,
"I've never found C so.
From where *I* stand, he seems to be
An uncompleted O."

C was vexed, "I'm much perplexed,
You criticise my shape.
I'm made like that, to help spell Cat
And Cow and Cool and Cape."

"He's right," said E; said F, "Whoopee!"
Said G, "'Ip, 'ip, 'ooray!"
"You're dropping me," roared H to G.
"Don't do it please I pray!"

"Out of my way," LL said to K.
"I'll make poor I look ILL."
To stop this stunt, J stood in front,
And presto! ILL was JILL.

"U know," said V, "that W
Is twice the age of me,
For as a Roman V is five
I'm half as young as he."

X and Y yawned sleepily,
"Look at the time!" they said.
"Let's all get off to beddy byes."
They did, then, "Z-z-z."

or

alternative last verse

X and Y yawned sleepily,
"Look at the time!" they said.
They all jumped in to beddy byes
And the last one in was Z!

LITTLE PIPPA

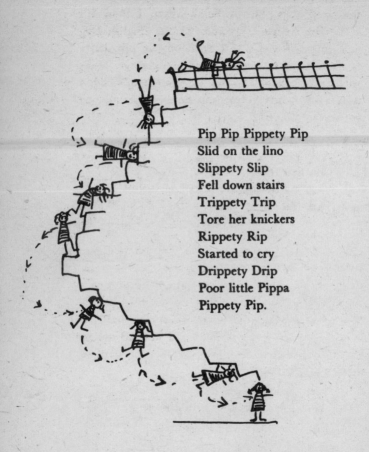

Pip Pip Pippety Pip
Slid on the lino
Slippety Slip
Fell down stairs
Trippety Trip
Tore her knickers
Rippety Rip
Started to cry
Drippety Drip
Poor little Pippa
Pippety Pip.

DOGS

Aristocrats have heirs, the poor have children, the rest keep dogs. The A Bomb apart, I think it's high time we paid attention to the English Dog cult, that now vies with Christianity for popularity in the top-ten religions. (Man, you're never alone with a Catholic.) The dog population of London is myriad, when you're not actually seeing one you're treading in it.

There was a time when the forebears of our contemporary dog ran free in packs of up to a hundred; short, stocky, yellow-haired fellows, hunting and living as they pleased, enjoying the primitive freedom of a collar-free throat. It's hard to believe that the lump of hairy fat, slobbed out in front of a Belgravia fire, is a direct descendant of those once noble creatures.

"Where walks Human there walks corruption."
So said somebody (I think it was me).

Back in the mists of time there fell from a tree
a half-upright hairy creature called Man. Later on
some were called Women, this eased the Palaeo-
lithic sexual frustration which up till then had been
called the Ice Age. (In my district it looks like
coming back, we had a beauty contest last week and
nobody won it.) Feasting on a mish-mash of mam-
moth, chips and Flag Sauce, early man moved on,
leaving in his wake a trail of bones, scrag ends and
unconscious batchelors who had overdone the
Spring fertility rites. Lying there, naked, daubed
with woad and with feathers in every orifice, they
looked, as we say, done up like a dog's dinner,
which in fact they became. From then on, the
more wayward of the dog pack scavenged in the
van of the itinerant early tribes. In the cold winter
of his discontent, man, by striking trees with
lightning invented (a) Fire and (b) Nothing else.
Wayward dog drew near the crackling flames and
warmed his body in the effulgent warmth. Unwittingly he was taking the first steps to a lush life
of social elevation and canine oblivion. Dog grew
sleeker, fatter, his fleas became an affluent society;
dog even learned to wag his tail. It seemed to
please his master, but always puzzled the dog. His
bitch bore a litter of twelve yellow flop-eared,
wobbly pups.

Now it came to pass that among the busy tribes there were many, shall we say, less industrious females. One such lass came upon what, up till then, had been a perfectly happy litter. She bent down (a dangerous pastime in that period) and picked up one of the pups. "Awwwwwwwwwwwwwwwwww," she said. From that moment on, the creature called Dog was doomed. Through the ensuing centuries he has been interbred, crossbred, inbred, overbred, stretched, reduced, lengthened, shortened, his face pushed in to make his eyes pop, hair over his eyes to blind him, tails lopped off, ears clipped, and latterly, fired to the moon.

Today, the creature has lost all knowledge of what he really is; the saving grace is the Mongrel (thank God for him!) who is of course shunned by the Canine Heirarchy. The female adulation of the dog puzzled many sociologists, then Freud made it clear: "What you can't impose on a man, you can always impose on a dog" (and vice versa), and "It's his own bloody fault" (that word now has Royal assent).

Nowadays, the neurotic descendants of the once wild dog can be seen in Royal Parks being escorted by white pinched-faced, blue-rinsed dowagers, that, or ensconsed in the back of a Rolls Bentley, with the window down to allow the beast freedom to bark at us less fortunate pavement travellers, and/or, under tables in expensive restaurants where they crunch the ankles of passing waiters and collect scraps of scampi from the plate of the owner ("Oh no, no sauce tartar for *him*").

Since 1945, a bundle of yapping nerves with hair on, called a Poodle, has become the status symbol of the top OK people. Shorn in the most grotesque

manner, this breed sports manicured claws, shampooed coats with champagne rinses, little leather bootees, and, the latest from America, an electrically-heated doggy jacket, the wire built into the lead, and the batteries, complete with thermostat, in the owner's handbag. Industries exclusively devoted to the canine gourmet are quoted on the stock exchange; on ITV "Don't let *your* dog eat the same scraps your husband has to, give him Woof-A, the dog food with the built in linger longer hormone vitamin", and in Queensway (I could hardly believe it), "Make your dog happy with 'The Meat flavoured Nylon Play-Bone'." This is the real stuff of humanity. How about "Milk flavoured wood chips for the starving children in the Congo", eh?

Miniatures. These are dogs that at one time stood fourteen foot high and have through the centuries been reduced to a convenient size to insert in pockets, handbags, shopping baskets. They are very rarely encouraged to walk; of course some of the better breeds aren't allowed to. You can see the whole lunatic menagerie any morning

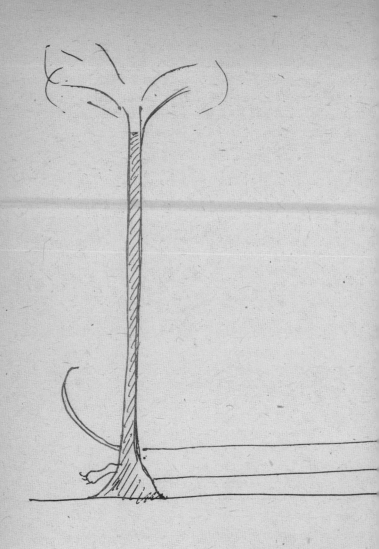

I think that I shall never see
A poem lovely as a tree.

after ten-thirty in the vicinity of the Round Pond, Kensington. While little children are being strapped down in prams, incarcerated in reins, sat on, hit, shouted at and generally terrorised, dogs are allowed to bite, chew, leap at old ladies, terrify, eat wild ducks, copulate and urinate at will, and sometimes on him (I spelt his name with a small w as he wishes to remain anonymous). All these cavortings are watched by the adoring owners who pass little maternal messages—"I *do* like him to play with dogs of his own age" and/or, "Have you put his name down for *Crufts* yet?" and of course, "He knows *every word you say*".

Will I ever forget the spectacle, that fine spring morning, when opposite Horse Guards Barracks an off-white Mercedes, suffering from Diplomatic Immunity, pulled to a Teutonic halt, a chauffeur opened the back door and, from a cushion, picked up what I can only describe as a piece of knotted string with legs. Carrying it like the crown jewels, he crossed Rotten Row and deposited the creature on the grass, where it sat for an hour blinking in the unaccustomed sunlight. From the rear window of the car, a doting, aging Brünnhilde watched its every move through a pair of opera glasses. One's spirits soar at this gesture of man's selfless devotion to his dog.

What happens to this vivacious collection of thoroughbreds when they age?

On grim winters' evenings, when streets are deserted, through the back alleys of Knightsbridge and Kensington, you will see two shadowy figures moving painfully down a dark street. They move painfully, and arthritically in the gloom. One is a fat, waddling, wheezy dog, one-time champion, now a grey-muzzled, dim-eyed has-been and, walking ten respectful paces behind him, another grey-muzzled, dim-eyed has-been of a man, both are the discards of one woman. Sadly they tread the pavements. In their wake usually follows a series of small posters, "£5 will be imposed on the owner of any dog that is allowed to foul the pavements" (as I read it, anyone can get away with it except the dog). Back home the blue-purple hair-rinsed madame is bending down to pick up a new black poodle puppy. "Awwwwwwwwwwwwwwwwww," she says. And that's where I came in.

"What are those people upstairs doing?"
(Also Showing Modern British Plumbing)

BUMP!

Things that go "bump!" in the night,
Should not really give one a fright.
It's the hole in each ear
That lets in the fear,
That, and the absence of light!

"That page looks quieter!"

ARITHMETIC

One and one are two,
  Two and two are four.
I only wish to goodness
  There wasn't any more!

Adding and subtracting,
  Really, what's the use?
When Winston Churchill was at school
  They say he was a goose.

Yet he became Prime Minister
  And help'd us win the war.
That's 'cause he didn't waste his time
  On two and two are four.

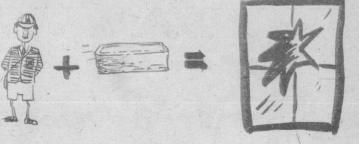

"I'll attack by sea."

"Wait till he gets near, then fire!"

PROTEST!

I must raise a protesting voice
    Against shopping in a Rolls-Royce.
I saw a lady in the Kensington Gore
    Drive her Rolls to a grocer's door.
All she bought was a dozen eggs!
When I go shopping
I travel on legs!

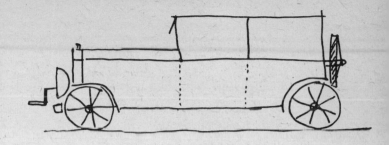

WRONG!

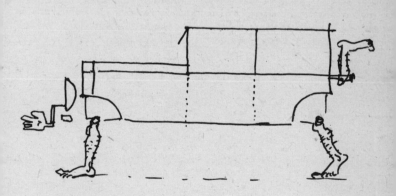

WRIGHT

DR DAVID MANTLE

Dr David Mantle *went*
   to Bintle Bontle Boo
To see the tonsils of a man
   he hardly even knew.

Dr David Mantle *got*
   to Bintle Bontle Boo
And to the man with tonsils said,
   "How do you do you do?"

Say "Ahh!" said Dr Mantle *then!*
   "I can't believe it's true.
You have three tonsils hanging where
   there normally are two."

"Only three?" the patient said.
   "My My! What *shall* I do?
There should be fifty tonsils there.
   Oh dear! Tut-tut! Boo-hoo!"

Dr David Mantle fled
   from Bintle Bontle Boo.
"I think that man was mad," he said.
   And I agree. Do you?

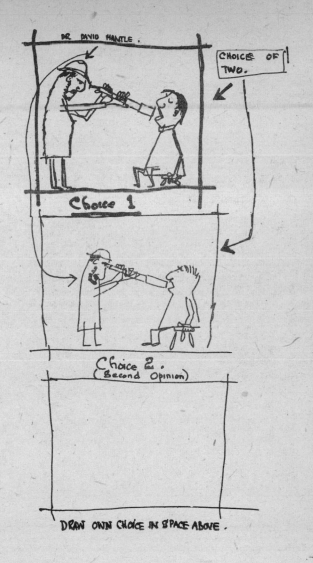

DR DAVID HANTLE.

CHOICE OF TWO.

Choice 1

Choice 2.
(Second Opinion)

DRAW OWN CHOICE IN SPACE ABOVE.

"Bet you can't do this!"

"It's my turn now, you've had two goes."

SAILOR JOHN

Johnny was a sailor lad who sailed the salty sea.
He loved to be on board a ship and feel the wind blo' free!

But then one day a storm blew up. The waves were ten feet high!

"All hands on deck!" The cry went up. "Or we are doomed to die!"

But Johnny was a sailor brave. "Don't worry lads," cried he,

"I'll show you how to save a ship from going down at sea."

RETURN TO SORRENTO *(3rd Class)*

I must go down to the sea again,
To the lonely sea and the sky,
I left my vest and socks there,
I wonder if they're dry?

CARRINGTON BRIGGS

Carrington Briggs
Cared not two figs
Whether he lived or died.
But when he was dead
He lay on his bed
And he cried, and cried, and cried.

YE TORTURES

From a document found in the Archives of Bude Monastery during a squirting excavation. It shows a complete list of tortures, approved by the Ministry of Works in the year 1438, for failure to pay leg tithe, or sockage.

The prisoner will be:

Bluned on ye Grunions
    and krelled on his Grotts
Ye legges will be twergled
    and pulled thru' ye motts!

His Nukes will be Fongled
    split thrice on yon Thulls
Then laid on ye Quottle
    and hung by ye Bhuls!

Twice thocked on the Phneffic,
    Yea broggled thrice twee.
Ye moggs will be grendled
    and stretched six foot three!

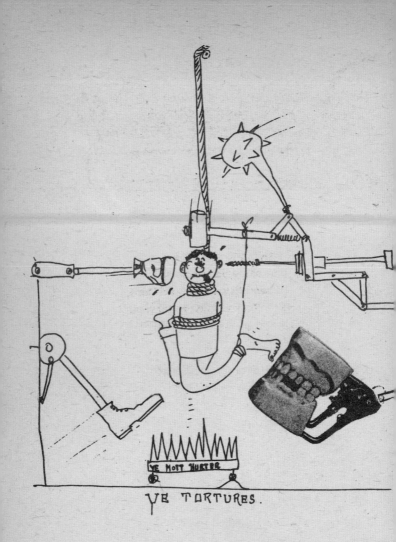

YE TORTURES.

By now, if ye victim
    show not ye sorrow,
Send him home. Tell him,
    "Come back to-morrow."

Never let your right hand know what your left middle hand is doing.
J. Anon.

"The genius of the British has always been originality."
Mr Macmillan, Tory Rally, May 2, 1951.

KNEES

Always keep your knees in front!
　　Don't let them slide behind!
Knees that get behind you
　　Are difficult to find!

Little Jim let his knees go!
　　They got *behind* the lad!
In Church he knelt down back to front
　　And made the vicar sad.

They bound his knees up with a strap,
　　And faced them to the front
And to this day—they face that way
　　* "Et gloria ducunt!"

* I don't know what it means but it rhymes. s.m.

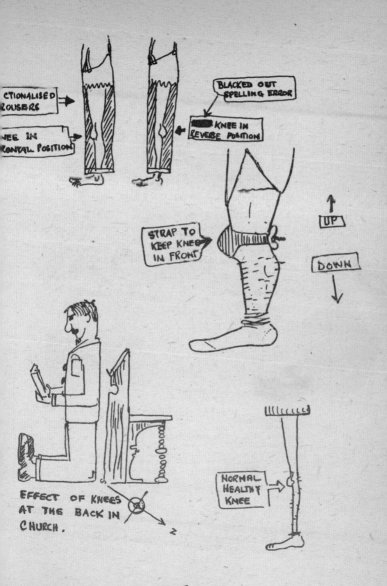

SECTIONALISED TROUSERS →

KNEE IN FRONTAL POSITION →

BLACKED OUT SPELLING ERROR

← KNEE IN REVESE POSITION

STRAP TO KEEP KNEE IN FRONT →

UP

DOWN

EFFECT OF KNEES AT THE BACK IN CHURCH.

NORMAL HEALTHY KNEE →

No. 1—Six Royal Eyes.

Total value of Prizes, £11 6s. 6d.

Whose may they be? Well, our readers shall apportion them, as far as they can, to their proper owners; and we, on our part, will

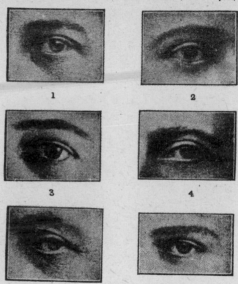

examine the lists they send in to us, and award Prizes as follows for successful results :—

First Prize—Silver Watch, value £3 3 0
Second Prize—Pair 18-carat Gold Links, value £2 2 0
Third Prize—A Year's Subscription to the *Graphic*, value £1 17 6
Four Extra Prizes—Silver Calendar and Compass Charm
    in each case, value £1 1 0

"I'll be glad when this dam' competition is over."

QUESTIONS, QUISTIONS & QUOSHTIONS

Daddy how does an elephant feel
When he swallows a piece of steel?
Does he get drunk
And fall on his trunk
Or roll down the road like a wheel?

Daddy what would a pelican do
If he swallowed a bottle of glue?
Would his beak get stuck
Would he run out of luck
And lose his job at the zoo?

Son tell me tell me true,
If I belted you with a shoe,
Would you fall down dead?
Would you go up to bed?
—Either of those would do.

LOBSTER

Libster Lobster
Labster Lee,
Living in
The deep blue sea.

Libster Lobster
Where are you?
Gone to lunch
(—Back at two).

Sir Keith Prowse (in Arab costume)
contemplating the slogan

"We have the best seats . . ."

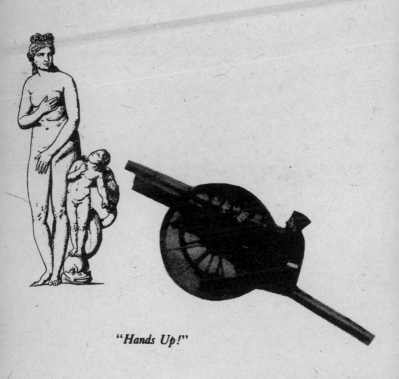

"Hands Up!"

"Where's 'e gon wif that gun?"

TELEPHONES

The discovery of the telephone came about by accident. In 1873 a young, spotty research chemist, called Dr MacTomjim, had left a plate of virus mould culture on the window-sill to cool before serving and, absent-mindedly, forgot it. Next morning as he was counting the dead children around it, eureka! Whereas the mould had originally been white, there, looming in the middle was an ominous black shape. At first the Doctor thought it was an illegal Jamaican immigrant with a wondrous new way of entering the U.K. But no, closer inspection showed it to be the first telephone. Unaware of his great discovery, the Doctor placed it up on a shelf and forgot it. How then, you say, did he discover it by accident? I'll tell you. It fell on his head.

His devoted Bronte-like wife, who up till then was happily vivisecting away removing the eyes from live rabbits etc., etc., rushed to her beloved's side. Seeing the bruise on his head, she swooned to

the floor. There, seeing the telephone, she swooned upright and *instinctively* dialled POLICE—FIRE—AMBULANCE. In a trice the police arrived, set fire to the doctor and drove away in an ambulance. Friends, the telephone had arrived!

The first telephone proved to be useless until the arrival of the second. It rapidly became the status symbol of the Industrial Nouveau Riche. Daguerrotypes show important men posing alongside their new telephones; families grouped lovingly *around* their telephones; generals pointing to their military telephones. Tunesmiths wrote "Will Willy tinkle Tilly on the Telephone Tonight". No play was complete without a telephone in the first act. It was a boon to the atrocious plays and playwrights that fouled the English stage from 1926 to '38. Soon millionaires were ordering ornate Victorian-rococo telephones of satin brass and glazed steel. The Czar of all the Russias commanded the famed Romanov court jeweller, Fabergé, to fashion a telephonic masterpiece. Made of pure Irish gold, inlaid with lapis lazuli taken from the tomb of

Tutankamen, and blazing with rare Australian fire opals, it caused the fiend Rasputin to say of it, "This is a great day for Russia!" It turned out he was right, they shot him. (He died defiantly singing "Anything you can do I kon do better".)

In British West Pongoland, warring Zulu chiefs were placated with great crates of Victorian telephones. It was common fare to see two chieftans sitting two feet apart talking to each other on the new "White Magic"; while outside, a snide British Lieutenant was hurriedly running up a Union Jack, and claiming the flagpole for the Queen, (back home Prince Albert had gone one better, he was claiming the Queen).

Effect of unsupervised GPO work in Buckingham Palace. Showing the famed short telephone lead.

Henry Irving boosted the sale of telephones with his play *The Bells*: the morning after the first night the G.P.O. was beseiged with applications for second night tickets. One man resented the intrusion of the instrument; William McGonagall, self-appointed Poet Laureate, and idiot, wrote:

What a sinful thing is the electrified telephone,
Such a disgrace hitherto before has never
been known,
I would rather see those to whom I speak,
Otherwise, for all I know I may be speaking
to a freak.

The tintinabulation of the Bells, drove Poe insane; he stabbed himself to death with a state-controlled raven. With good reason; the G.P.O. phone bell could be heard three miles away as the crow flies, and is the direct cause of deafness among crows today. This nerve-shattering bell is the same one installed at the bedsides of wax-frail old ladies in private nursing homes. Now, by shorting the circuit in the early hours, mercenary doctors in need of bed space can set off a carillon that reaps a fine crop of Coronary Occulisions.

My first phone was a "party" line, that is, when your T.V., radio, wife and mistress break down, you can pick up the phone and listen to the neighbours. It soon became a burden. One of my writers would phone me at midnight, and indulge

in seeing how far he could walk away from the phone and still be heard; last time he got as far as King's Road, Chelsea, where he was knocked down by a bus.

My friend Mr Sellers had it bad. He installed a phone in his car. Rather than let it lie idle all night, he would drive into the Kentish Weald and phone back to tell his mother he was "Out". It was becoming evident to me that the phone was a drug, and vieing with cigarettes for cancer of the inner ear.

Victim: Doctor, I've *got* to have more phone calls.

Dr: But Mrs Leigh, you're up to seventy a day!

Victim: I know. I've tried to cut them down but I can't.

Dr: Very well Mrs Leigh. Do you want them on the G.P.O. or do you want to be phoned privately.

Victim: My husband is rich.

Dr: Very well, I want you to ring this number ten times a day after meals.

I invited a fellow sufferer to dine with me. To music by Debussy, and candlelight, we sat down. As we commenced soup, the phone in the next room rang. My guest stiffened, half rose and dropped his spoon. For a moment he listened. "Aren't you going to answer it?" he said, his voice strangely castrati. "We never answer the telephone on Fridays, we are Catholics, and the Jews next door are watching us." My guest was now quite pale, trembling, and his wig had slipped. "Would you like me to answer it for you?" he whined from his foetus position on the floor. I pointed a threatening obstetrical finger at him but, half-crazed by the bells, he ran screaming to the phone. Lifting the handset he received the following message, "Your soup's getting cold you silly B----r." It had all been prearranged twixt me and a certain Mr Secombe.

Which brings us to the promoters of this malaise, those faceless sons of fun, the G.P.O.! Who from time to time issue little pain-killing brochures telling of fresh G.P.O. triumphs in a world of absolutely no competition. "VALUE FOR MONEY" says their latest bit of bumph, "When you pick up your telephone, you have a thousand million pounds worth of equipment at your fingertips." That's O.K. with me man, what I complain about are those five-pound-a-week brains that answer them.

Entry of GPO engineers into new home.

People who live in glass houses
Should pull the blinds
When removing their trousers.

"Come out with your hands up"

WRENKLED STRIN

(The Author freely admits he has kno knowledge of Wrenkled Strin. *Ed.*)

ROUND AND ROUND

Small poem based upon my daughter's (6) remarks on overhearing me tell her brother Sean (4½) that the world was going round. (Australia, June-July, 1958.)

One day a little boy called Sean
(Age four) became profound.
He asked his dad
If it were true
The world was going round.

"Oh yes, that's true," his daddy said
"It goes round night and day."
"Then doesn't it get tired dad?"
Young Sean was heard to say.

His sister in the bath called out
"What did dad say—what did he?"
He said "The world is going round."
Said she "Well it's making me giddy!"

"TIT-BITS" SYSTEM OF LIFE INSURANCE.

SIXTEEN CLAIMS HAVE BEEN PAID.

ONE HUNDRED POUNDS WILL BE PAID BY THE OCEAN, RAILWAY, AND GENERAL ACCIDENT ASSURANCE COMPANY, LIMITED, MANSION HOUSE BUILDINGS, LONDON, TO THE PERSON WHOM THE PROPRIETOR OF "TIT-BITS" MAY DECIDE TO BE THE NEXT-OF-KIN OF ANYONE WHO IS KILLED IN A RAILWAY ACCIDENT IN THE UNITED KINGDOM, PROVIDED A COPY OF THE CURRENT ISSUE OF "TIT-BITS" IS FOUND UPON THE DECEASED AT THE TIME OF THE CATASTROPHE. THIS SUM WILL NOT BE PAID IN THE CASE OF AN ACCIDENT TO A RAILWAY SERVANT WHEN ON DUTY, OR OF A SUICIDE.

"And not one of us with the current issue."

BLAST THE MAN!

There was a man called Hermoniges Phniggs,
Who lived in Kilburn in terrible digs,
He changed his name to Eric Fruit,
And now it won't rhyme.

Phniggs,
Digs
Figs   = Fruit
Gigs
Jigs
Pigs
Wigs

WHO NOSE?

Oh what a thing is a nose.
It grows and it grows and it grows.
It grows on your head
While you're lying in bed,
At the opposite end to your toes.

Written by my brother
Desmond
(with my permission)

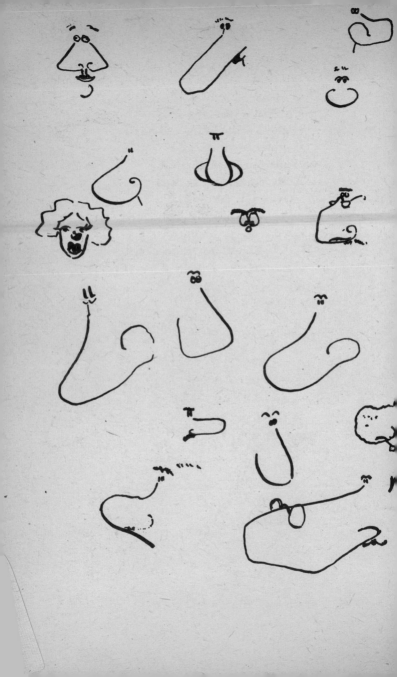

Site for Sore Eyes

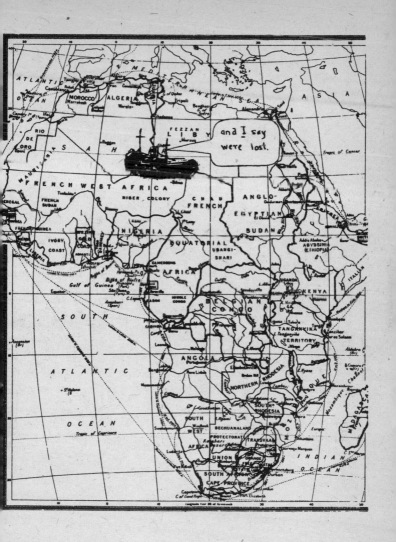

Running Out

The end

Wyndham Books are obtainable from many booksellers and newsagents. If you have any difficulty please send purchase price plus postage on the scale below to:

Wyndham Cash Sales,
PO Box 11,
Falmouth,
Cornwall

OR

Star Book Service,
G.P.O. Box 29,
Douglas,
Isle of Man,
British Isles.

While every effort is made to keep prices low, it is sometimes necessary to increase prices at short notice. Wyndham Books reserve the right to show new retail prices on covers which may differ from those advertised in the text or elsewhere.

Postage and Packing Rate
U.K.
One book 22p plus 10p per copy for each additional book ordered to a maximum charge of 82p.

B.F.P.O. & Eire
One book 22p plus 10p per copy for the next 6 books, and thereafter 4p per book.

Overseas
One book 30p plus 10p per copy for each additional book.

These charges are subject to Post Office fluctuations.